Joy Forever

Joy Marie Hallare

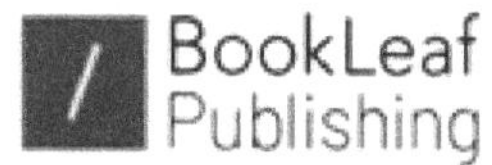

Presentation by *BookLeaf Publishing*

Web: www.bookleafpub.com

E-mail: info@bookleafpub.com

ISBN: 9789357213066

First edition 2023

Joy at Her Finest

Joy,

Glitter
Shine
In the limelight
Smile
Worth millions
Build confidence
Break the Roof
Shoot through the sky

Joy at Her Moment

Joy,

Be calm
Relax
Sit on the grass
Breath in
Breathe out
Imagine
Think
Visualize

What am I thinking?
What should I do?

Joy Opening Her Mind

Joy,

Observe
Pencil on my left hand
Notebook on my right

Turn the first page
Eyes closed
Imagine
Think
Visualize

Hello Joy

Welcome to my world
Welcome to my vision

Joy of Everything

Joy,

I smell food
Of thought
Food
Of love
Food
Of abundance

Arrival of Joy

Joy,

I smell
Energy
Drive
Upon
My arrival

Joy in Person

Joy,

I smell
My thick wavy curly hair
With a scent
Of strawberry,
Honey,
And coconut

I smell
My chocolate
Mocha skin
Standing
In front of
The sun
Feet on the sand
And fresh seawater
Around me

Joy at Home

Joy,

I smell
Lavender
When I rub ointment
On my neck
Filled with scars
And bruises

I smell
Mist
Of Jasmine
Around me
Nostalgia
From my parents'
Backyard
Filled with a garden of
Endless flowers
Blooming every spring

Sad Joy

Joy,

Cold
Frozen
Not feeling anything
No pain
No emotion

Nothing

Save Me Joy

Joy,

I cry
In agony
I hide
From everybody
I want to be alone
But I want
Someone
To save me

Crying Joy

I cry
In pain
when
I fall
and got back up

Happy Joy

Joy,

I cry
Happy
When I get
The results
I deserve
And worked
Hard for

Helping Joy

Joy,

I cry
Happy
When there's a
Helping hand and
An opportunity
For me
Welcoming me
To the light

Joy of Commitment

14

Joy,

My skin
Is tough
Filled with sweat
From perseverance
And dedication
Strength
To continue

Joy Inside

Joy,

My face
Filled with tears
From fears
Of her past,
Present,
And future

Touch Joy

Joy,

Warm
Comfort
Sleep
Next to me
Sing a
Lullaby
Kiss on my forehead
Dream

Speak Joy

Joy,

Stand up
For friends
Who had no voice

Speak Joy

Joy,

Soothe
Someone
At their worst

Speak Joy

Joy,

Speak
From the
bottom
of your heart

Say Joy

Breathe
Inhale
Exhale
Say
something

Joy Forever

Joy,

I see Joy
I feel Joy
I hear Joy
I speak Joy
I touch Joy

Forever
I am
Free

www.ingramcontent.com/pod-product-compliance
Lightning Source LLC
LaVergne TN
LVHW021349200726
843509LV00014B/2756